BUSINESS PORTRAITS

BOEING

Published by VGM Career Horizons,
a division of NTC Publishing Group,
4255 West Touhy Avenue
Lincolnwood (Chicago), Illinois 60646-1975, U.S.A.

Gould, William
VGM's business portraits: Boeing/William Gould.
p. cm. – (VGM's business portraits)
Includes index.
Summary: Introduces basic business concepts, using Boeing Corporation as a case study.
ISBN 0-8442-4775-8
1. Boeing Company – Juvenile literature. 2. Aircraft industry – United States – Juvenile literature. (1. Boeing Company. 2. Aircraft industry.) I. Title. II. Series.
HD9711.U63B6329 1996
338.7′629133′0973-dc20 95-51649
CIP
AC

Manufactured in Belgium by Proost International Book Production.

BUSINESS PORTRAITS

BOEING

WILLIAM GOULD

95
VGM Career Horizons
a division of *NTC Publishing Group*
Lincolnwood, Illinois USA

ACKNOWLEDGMENT

Our thanks to The Boeing Company for providing us with copies of their annual reports and historical publications from which we drew information to develop a profile of the company. Editorial comments made and conclusions reached by the author about general business practices of international companies do not necessarily reflect the policies and practices of The Boeing Company.

CONTENTS

▲ Businesses need people (human resources), things (physical resources) and money (capital).

▼ A business uses money to buy human and physical resources, and create a product or service which it sells for a profit.

The adventure of business

Business often sounds difficult but its basic principles are simple, and it can be very exciting. The people involved in the creation and running of the businesses we examine in VGM's BUSINESS PORTRAITS faced challenges and took risks that make some adventure stories seem dull.

What is a business?

If you sell your old football to a friend for money you are making a business deal. Anyone who produces goods or services in return for money, or works for an organization that does so, is involved in business.

Businesses try to make profits. They try to sell things for more than the amount the things cost them to make. They usually invest part of the profit they make to produce and sell more of their products. If they have no money to invest, they may borrow it.

The language of business

Many of the technical terms that make the language of business sound complicated are explained on pages 46 and 47.

Business matters

Yellow panels throughout the book explain general business concepts. Blue panels tell you more about Boeing.

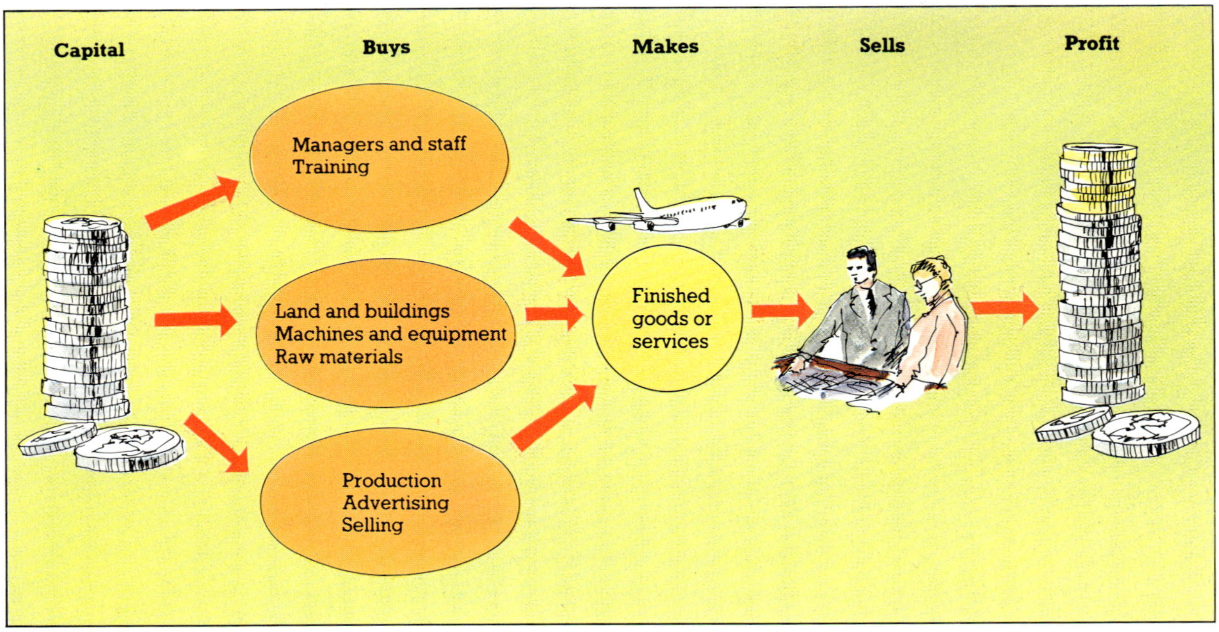

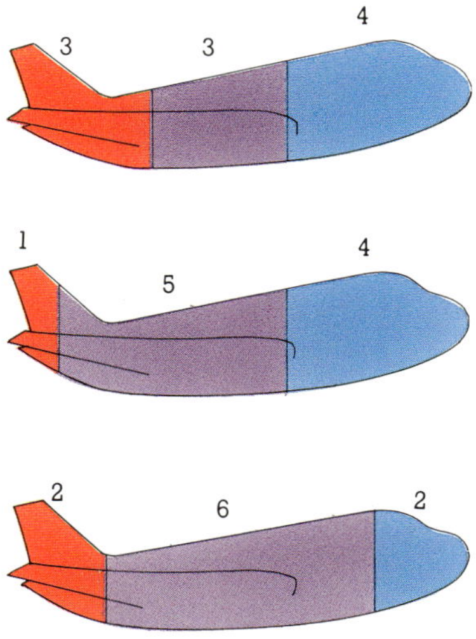

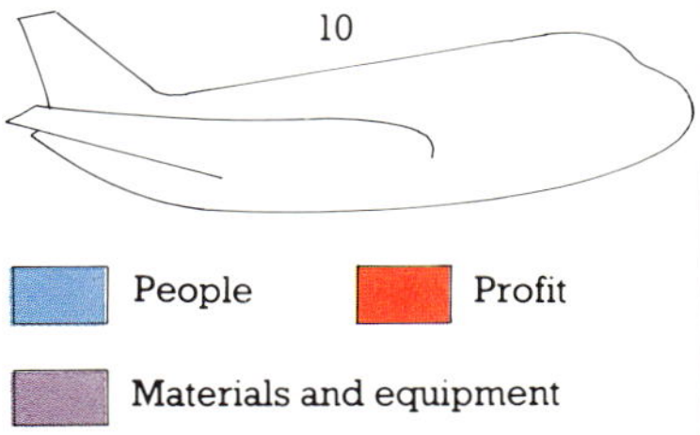

◀ The purpose of a business is to make a profit. Profit is the amount of money earned from sales that remains after all the costs (people plus materials and equipment) are paid. The higher the costs, the lower the profits. If a plane sells for $10 million and costs $8 million to make, the profit is $2 million.

The business of Boeing

Every day about 2.5 million passengers travel on aircraft manufactured by The Boeing Company. Boeing is the world's most important aerospace company. More than 400 airlines fly its aircraft and the United States government relies on it for military planes, systems and space vehicles. Throughout the world, around 117,000 people work directly for Boeing and thousands more indirectly. If you have ever flown on an airplane, the chances are that it will have been a Boeing.

BOEING FACTS

* Headquarters is in the Puget Sound area of Seattle, Washington.
* Commercial Airplane Group employs 70,000 people; Defense and Space 30,000; Computer Services 7,000
* Staff salaries and benefits are around $6 billion.
* In 1994 Boeing's sales were worth $22 billion.
* Thirteenth largest corporation in the US.
* In 1994 foreign sales totalled $12 billion.
* Fifty per cent of its sales are made overseas.

▼ The Boeing Company has three operating divisions.

Commercial Airplanes

* Manufactures civil aircraft.
* Customers include airlines, governments and other organizations.
* Gives aftersales support to 500 airlines round the world.

Defense and Space

* Manufactures military airplanes and helicopters, missiles and rockets, electronic weapons-guidance and warning systems.
* Customers include the US government, overseas governments and NASA.

Computer Services

* Provides the company with advanced computer technology.
* Customers include the other two groups and government customers.

Flying – transport of the future

In 1903 Orville and Wilbur Wright made the first powered flight at Kitty Hawk in North Carolina. In those days few would have believed that one day people would regard travelling by air as casually as travelling by bus.

At the time William Boeing was setting himself up in the timber business in the great forest region of the Pacific Northwest. From 1908 he was based in Seattle, Washington. His business was successful and he made enough money to take an active interest in flying. His friend Thomas F. Hamilton was the first man to fly an airplane in Seattle. Boeing took his first flight in 1914. He enjoyed it so much that the following year he took flying lessons and bought his own seaplane. In an area with many huge lakes and few airfields, seaplanes were more practical than conventional aircraft.

WILLIAM E. BOEING

William Edward Boeing (1881-1956) was born in Detroit, into a hardworking German immigrant family with interests in the timber trade. In 1902 he dropped out of Yale University, moved to Seattle, and made his own fortune in timber. From 1916 he devoted himself to aircraft. He led his expanding empire until 1934, when government legislation forced the company to be broken up. Boeing retired in bitterness. He sold his aviation business and turned to deep-sea fishing and breeding livestock.

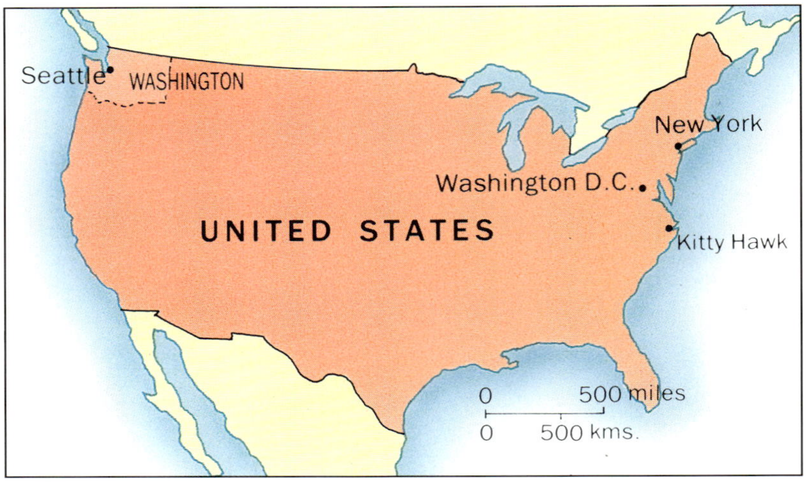

▶ In 1903 the Wright brothers made their historic flight at Kitty Hawk, North Carolina. Few people in Washington State had even seen an aircraft when Boeing built his first seaplane.

Boeing gets going

Flying made a great hobby, but Boeing could see the commercial possibilities in flight. There were few good roads in his part of the United States, just mile after mile of forest, lake and wilderness. Through Hamilton, Boeing met G. Conrad Westervelt, a young naval officer who was as keen on flying as he was. The two decided to design and build their own seaplane. They founded a company called Pacific Aero Products and built a prototype on the shore of Lake Union. It was finished by early 1916.

▲ The B & W Seaplane, Boeing's first product.

BUSINESS MATTERS: CAPITAL

In order to start a business, you generally need money. You have to buy raw materials, pay staff, rent or buy premises and equipment, pay to sell your product, and pay yourself. This money is called capital. As well as cash, it includes the value of the company's assets – everything it owns from furniture to unsold goods. William Boeing was lucky. He had his father's money to start his timber business, and the wealth from this first business to finance his second.

Building a plane

Today aircraft are made of aluminium. In the early days they were built of wood, wire and linen. Boeing's first plane, the B&W (Boeing and Westervelt) Seaplane was built not by engineers and assembly-line workers but by shipwrights, carpenters and seamstresses. Like most airplanes before 1930, it was a biplane, with two sets of wings, one above the other. It took off and landed on water by means of two large floats in place of wheels.

Boeing thought that the B&W, with a top speed of 120 km/h (75 mph), was a great improvement on existing aircraft. He hoped that the US Navy would buy the seaplane, but he was disappointed. Fortunately, he had plenty of money from his timber business to keep the business running.

Paying the bills

Boeing had a staff of 24. The lowest wage was 14 cents an hour, the highest – for pilots – was about $300 a month. Boeing had to find $700 a week to pay the staff. In addition, he had to buy the wood and other raw materials to make the planes and rent a factory in which to build them.

War and peace

▲ **World War I planes were flimsy and dangerous. Few survived more than three or four combats.**

BUSINESS MATTERS: INVESTMENT

Unlike William Boeing, most people do not have a personal fortune. If they have a good idea for a business, they have to save up enough money themselves or borrow money from someone else. Many individuals and organizations, such as banks and other businesses, are willing to lend money to people starting up a business, if they think the business will make money. Their loans will be repaid with interest, and often they are able to share the new company's profits in exchange for the money they risked in the first place.

Boeing did not have long to wait for success. In 1917, the United States entered World War I, which had been going on in Europe since 1914. The fighting was mostly carried on by men in trenches with machine guns. Aircraft were used for reconnaissance, and often became involved in "dogfight" battles in the sky. One small plane would line itself up behind an enemy plane and attempt to bring it down with machine-gun fire.

Boeing's company, now renamed the Boeing Airplane Company, soon found itself building military training aircraft and flying boats for the navy. One order was for 50 Model C training aircraft, the first all-Boeing design. Like other aircraft manufacturers, Boeing was doing well out of the war.

The war's over

Within 18 months, the war was over. No more planes were needed and the government cancelled its military contracts. To an aircraft manufacturer, peace does not always mean prosperity. For Boeing, it was almost a disaster. Aircraft left over from the war flooded the market. Nobody wanted a new plane. William Boeing kept his company going by building boats and furniture. He cut the staff to two and paid the bills out of his own money. His huge factory lay empty.

▲ William Boeing (right) and his pilot partner Eddie Hubbard used a Model C-700 for the first international airmail service.

Carrying the mail

Gradually, Boeing's will to succeed led him in another direction. Carrying mail across country by road or rail took time. By air it was swift, and people wanted their mail to get there quicker. Boeing seized the opportunity. He built a flying boat to carry airmail between Seattle and Vancouver in Canada – the first international airmail service. Internal airmail services were controlled by the government.

◀ Carpenters, joiners and sailmakers were key workers in the first Boeing factory. Design, engineering and production were supervised by Clairmont L. Egtvedt, Tsu Wong and Philip G. Johnson.

BUSINESS MATTERS: ENTERPRISE AND RISK

The word *enterprise* can be used to mean a project or business venture or a company. The word also means inventiveness, originality and the willingness to take a risk in something you believe in. Taking a risk is often bad sense because it can lead to failure, but sometimes it can bring success. If you see an opportunity, a need that nobody else has spotted, you can make money by being the first to seize it. It makes sense to take a risk only if your business can afford to lose the money it costs.

▲ The badge of Boeing Air Transport Inc, one of several subsidiary companies of the Boeing group. Others included engine manufacturers Pratt & Whitney, propeller maker Hamilton and the aircraft companies Chance, Vought, Stearman and Sikorsky.

▶ The last word in luxury air travel was available to passengers on the Model 80: reading lamps, ventilators, leather seats and toilets with hot and cold water.

Airline pioneers

In 1927 the government opened up airmail routes inside the United States to private operators. This gave Boeing a further opportunity to expand. The company had long before resumed making military aircraft and was making money. The planes that carried the mail also carried passengers, so Boeing became an airline operator, called United Air Lines, as well as an aircraft manufacturer.

Boeing's company carried passengers and mail between Chicago and San Francisco and between Seattle and Los Angeles. By merging with other companies Boeing expanded his business into a huge airline and manufacturing company called the United Aircraft and Transport Corporation (UATC).

BUSINESS MATTERS: BUYING AND MERGING

When a market is expanding, when more and more people wish to buy a particular product or service, companies try to grab as much business as they can. They merge with or buy each other in order to grow more quickly. It takes a lot of time to develop new products, and you may be able to buy a company that is already producing what you want on the spot for much the same money. In the 1920s, Boeing bought or merged with one company after another, so that it rapidly became a giant and seized a huge slice of the market. Businesses can do this only if they are making a lot of money or are able to borrow the money and pay it back in due course with interest.

Going public

In order to finance this expansion Boeing raised capital by issuing shares. This is known as going public, because members of the public, along with businesses and other institutions, can buy shares and own part of the company.

BUSINESS MATTERS: STOCKS AND SHARES

A business may raise money by issuing shares. As their name suggests, shares are a share in a company. A group of shares is called stock. The owners of the company sell a set number of shares in the business. If the company makes large profits, the value of the shares will go up. If the company does badly, the price of the shares will fall and shareholders will want to get rid of them.

As well as the value of the shares rising and falling, the shareholders may receive a payment called a dividend. When the company adds up how much profit it has made at the end of the year, it keeps what it needs to spend in the future and shares out a certain amount among the shareholders. If the company has a bad year, there are no dividends. If the company fails completely, the shares become worthless.

BUSINESS MATTERS: GOOD DESIGN

Early on Boeing told his staff, "Our job is to keep everlastingly at research and experiment, to adapt our laboratories to production as soon as practicable, to let no new improvement in flying and flying equipment pass us by." This enthusiasm for experimentation and innovation is one of the main reasons for The Boeing Company's success. From the start its designers worked to overcome great technical problems, and the company was always willing to spend money on research because it recognized the importance of good design.

Achievements in design

In 1930 Boeing changed the shape of aircraft forever by producing the first single-engine all-metal monoplane. Unlike earlier biplanes with two sets of wings, the Monomail was streamlined, which enabled it to fly faster. It had an engine cowling to reduce drag and landing gear that could be drawn into the aircraft during flight. It set a standard for modern aircraft that was followed by the twin-engined B-9 bomber and the B-247.

▼ The Monomail carried mail and passengers. Its streamlined design was revolutionary.

▲ **Boeing's engineers had to learn new techniques with the change from wood to metal. Training staff is important in any business.**

Breaking up

The B-247, developed in 1933, was the first modern airliner. Based on the Monomail, it carried passengers in speed and comfort, carving $7\frac{1}{2}$ hours off the flight time from New York to Los Angeles. Boeing Air Transport (part of UATC) ordered 60 off the drawing board at a cost of $60,000 each, and 15 more were sold abroad. Trans World Airlines (TWA) tried to order B-247s, too, but UATC declined the order because they could not fulfil it. TWA went to Boeing's rival Douglas and they developed the DC-2, a superior design that eclipsed the 247.

An unexpected blow

In 1934 the United States government passed a law that made it illegal for aircraft manufacturers to have a financial stake in any airline that had a contract to carry mail. This was devasting for William Boeing. It meant that the business he had built up would have to be disbanded, and its separate parts sold off.

The company split into three parts: United Air Lines, and two manufacturing companies – United Aircraft Corporation and The Boeing Airplane Company. William Boeing was so disheartened by what he saw as unfair government interference that he left the company.

DESIGN FOR THE FUTURE

Based on the Monomail, the 247 (right) was the first twin-engined transport plane. Its basic design is still in use today. It had an all-metal fuselage with retractable wheels, two cantilever wings, two supercharged engines encased in smooth cowlings, and variable-pitch propellers. It had de-icer "boots" on the wings and tail, a crew cabin for two pilots and a stewardess, and a ten-seater passenger cabin. Unfortunately for Boeing, Douglas produced a superior design in the DC-2, and followed it with the DC-3 (inset), called the Dakota. This was so fast, smooth, economical and reliable that it became the world's leading airliner. By 1945, 13,000 had been made.

Bigger and better

With its founder gone, and no passengers or mail to transport, Boeing concentrated on building aircraft, designing them to the highest standards to meet the increasing demand. The new chairman, Clairmont L. Egtvedt, was an engineer and draughtsman. Under his guidance Boeing produced larger, more luxurious planes. For people who wanted to cross the oceans by air, the company built the Model 314 flying boat, the first long-haul ocean-crossing airliner. It was nicknamed the "Clipper" after the great ocean-going sailing ships.

BUSINESS MATTERS: GROWTH

Knowing when and how to grow is one of the most difficult issues in business. Firms that grow slowly may miss out on vital profits and lose their share of the market to more aggressive competitors. Firms that grow quickly may have to borrow heavily and then fail to generate enough business to repay their loans.

▲ The 314 carried 74 passengers by day or 50 in overnight sleeping accommodation.

BUSINESS MATTERS: MONOPOLY AND COMPETITION

Businesses selling similar products or services are in competition with each other. Competition protects consumers. If only one company were to sell a particular product, it could charge as much as it liked regardless of the quality. It would have a monopoly. Competition allows people to choose the price and quality they want.

In order to protect competition, many governments forbid companies to become monopolies. They also prevent companies that sell similar products from fixing prices. Some people are opposed to these measures. They believe that private enterprise rather than government legislation can best protect customers.

Ups and downs

Passengers on board Pan American Clippers could cross the Atlantic or Pacific in style. Seated in a spacious dining salon, they could gaze out of picture windows while gourmet meals were served to them. There were dressing rooms, beds and even a bridal suite on board.

There was even greater luxury to be had on the Model 307 Stratoliner, for the plane had a major innovation. The cabin was pressurized, which meant that it could fly higher. Because air is thinner at high altitudes, planes use less fuel, which makes them cheaper to fly. They could also fly just "above the weather" which makes for less turbulence. Only 10 Stratoliners were built, however, because, in the late 1930s, a more terrible turbulence was threatening the world.

WILLIAM ALLEN

William Allen was Boeing's most senior lawyer before he became president and then chairman of the company. He guided the company from the pre-war age of propeller-driven aircraft into the space age, introducing jets, jumbo jets, rockets, missiles and spacecraft.

War and peace – again

With World War II (1939-45), history repeated itself for Boeing. The company put great effort into manufacturing vast numbers of two huge bombers, the B-17 Flying Fortress and the B-29 Superfortress. After the United States entered the war in 1941, Boeing put its factories in Seattle and Wichita, Kansas, on a war footing. In 1942 it built another plant near Seattle at Renton. At its wartime peak, Boeing employed 78,000 people.

▲ From 1935, the US war effort produced an astonishing 12,371 B-17 bombers. When the men went away to war, women worked on the assembly lines. At the height of production, in 1944, 16 aircraft were being built in a day.

▲ Built in secrecy to end the war in the Pacific, B-29s by the thousands bombed Japanese targets.

Then with peace came crisis. Military contracts ended, just as they had in 1918, and Boeing had to cut its staff to 8,000.

Postwar disappointments

Boeing's first postwar commercial plane, the Model 377 Stratocruiser, failed. It was a luxurious aircraft with seats on two decks, but it did not attract enough passengers. After the war, business in general was bad and few people could afford to travel in such style. Fortunately Boeing's last propeller-driven transport plane, the C-97 Stratofreighter, was popular with the US military as a troop carrier and mid-air refueller. This kept the company in business. William Allen, the company's new president, knew that the company would recover only if they could keep ahead of their rivals by using the very latest technology.

ENOLA GAY

A total of 3,970 B-29 Superfortresses were built before production ceased in 1946. On August 6, 1945, one named Enola Gay was selected to drop the first atomic bomb on Hiroshima, Japan. Three days later, a second B-29, the Bockscar, dropped another bomb on Nagasaki. Japan surrendered shortly afterwards.

BUSINESS MATTERS: BOOM AND BUST

Recession is a periodic decline in a nation's business activity. Fewer goods are bought, sold and produced. As a result fewer people are employed. Unemployed people have less money to spend on goods, so even fewer goods are produced and sold. During a recession, businesses try to cut their costs, increase productivity and use any means they can to raise demand. If they cannot, they may collapse completely and go bankrupt.

In boom times, when people have more money to spend, businesses flourish and grow because demand for their goods is high. Inflation occurs when prices rise and outstrip wages. Money loses its purchasing power, demand for goods drops and this triggers a recession.

The jet age

The introduction of jet-propelled aircraft towards the end of the war pointed the way forward for Boeing. The B-47 Stratojet bomber could fly at over 965 km/h (600mph). The US Air Force bought more than 2,000 Stratojets during the decade following its introduction. An even more successful bomber, still in service today, followed. It was the B-52.

One country that had bought the 377 Stratocruiser was Britain. Britain's de Havilland company had also developed a medium-range jet airliner called the Comet. Boeing knew that long-distance travel demanded the speed and cost-effectiveness that only jet aircraft could deliver.

ROLLOUT

When a ship is ready to sail for the first time, it is launched in a special ceremony. Aircraft are "launched" too in a ceremony called the rollout when the first completed aircraft is shown off. The rollout of the first 707 was an exciting event for Boeing.

The secret of success

Boeing decided to build a superior jet airliner – in secret. It announced that it would invest $16 million on a new project, named 367-80. This led people to think that an improved version of the Stratofreighter was on the way. In 1954 the prototype of the Boeing 707 (then named the Dash 80) was

▼ **The Dash 80 rolls out. The prototype 707 heralded a new era in jet transport. Many 707s are still flying.**

◀ The E-3A Airborne Warning and Control System is equipped with communications, navigation, data processing and display equipment, monitored by a military crew (inset).

SPY IN THE SKY

The E-3A AWACS (Airborne Warning and Control System) is a surveillance aircraft, equipped with radar, computers and advanced electronic communications systems. This sophisticated equipment is fitted on to the body of a 707. With its giant rotating disc aerial, it patrols the skies at about 10,000 meters (33,000 ft), watching and listening. Future AWACS will be mounted on 767s.

rolled out. It was a revolution – a passenger airliner that cut the journey time across the Atlantic by half and the cost of fares by almost as much. Flying at high altitudes to avoid the weather, the elegant Boeing 707 gave passengers a smooth, quiet flight. Thanks to the 707, air travel for business and pleasure became more common. The number of passenger journeys doubled.

During the 1960s Boeing produced three more jet airliners, all of which are still in service. The 727 is a short-to-medium-range jet, the 737 a short-range. Both planes have been far more successful than even their maker envisaged. Even more successful is the Boeing 747.

AIR FORCE ONE

Boeing prides itself on supplying the US president's personal aircraft. From 1958 until 1990, these were 707s, each equipped as an airborne White House, on which the president could travel in comfort and be as in touch with the world as he would be on the ground in Washington. There were also adequate facilities for visitors and journalists aboard. Since 1990, two even more luxurious and well-equipped 747-200s have served as Air Force Ones.

◀ The 737 is popular with package-tour operators.

▲ The vast engines of the 747-400 enable it to fly further and carry more passengers than any other commercial jetliner.

▼ The factory at Everett, Washington, where jumbo jets are assembled.

The jumbo jet age

With fares dropping, more and more people began to travel by air. In the 1960s British and French manufacturers decided that people wanted to reach their destinations quickly. They concentrated on building an aircraft that could fly people faster than the speed of sound. They produced the sleek, supersonic Concorde. It was a technological marvel, but also it was expensive, noisy and carried only a small number of passengers.

In America, Boeing's market researchers came to a different conclusion. People did want to go faster, but not at any cost. Most of all they wanted lower fares. By producing a bigger "wide-bodied" plane with more powerful engines, Boeing could carry more passengers further, and still go faster than most other subsonic airliners.

Success from the start

In March 1966, the board of directors of Boeing gave the go-ahead for the 747. Developing this mammoth aircraft would cost $1 billion. A factory big enough for it would cost

COLD-WAR WARHORSE

The 8-jet B-52 Stratofortress, which first flew in 1952, was the US Air Force's principal bomber for over 40 years. Built to carry nuclear weapons, it was used to rain down high explosives on the jungles of Vietnam.

$2 million. It was a massive risk, as much as the net worth of the company. But research showed that the plane was needed. A month after the decision to proceed, before the land for the factory had even been purchased, Pan American, the United States' leading airline, placed an order for 25 of the 747s at a cost of $20 million each. Other airlines also rushed to buy the jumbo. By the end of 1966, 11 airlines had ordered 88 planes. It was too late for Boeing's competitors. In the race for customers, Boeing had left its rivals far behind.

◀ **On the ground, the 747, with its wide, heavy body and huge flexing wings, looks as though it could never fly, but in the air it is smooth and graceful. The 1,000th 747 was rolled out in 1993.**

FIT TO FLY

Safety in aviation is vital. National and international organizations impose strict controls and regulations for aircraft and air traffic. In the United States the Federal Aviation Administration inspects every newly manufactured plane. An aircraft can fly only when it has been given a certificate of airworthiness, which states that the plane is in good flying condition. If anything goes wrong with an aircraft that might possibly put passengers in danger, all similar aircraft are grounded until safety checks have been carried out.

Rollout

By September 1968, when the first completed 747 was rolled out, 27 airlines had ordered the plane. In all, 158 jumbos had been ordered. The first 747 made its maiden flight on February 9, 1969. After rigorous ground and flight tests, the 747 received its certificate of airworthiness and entered service with Pan American on January 22, 1970. Since then, bigger and better versions of the original jumbo have come into service, and more than 80 airlines operate the plane.

Branching out

Although Boeing was the most successful aircraft company in the world, it had a potential problem. It had only one type of product. There would always be a need for new types of aircraft, but the demand for them would vary. There were also other companies in the market. Suppose someone produced better aircraft, and Boeing could not sell theirs? With low sales, would come low profits. People would lose their jobs and the company might fail, even though it had been so successful. All companies with only one type of product face this possibility.

Surviving bad times

From 1945 onwards, Boeing developed missiles, space equipment, helicopters and computer services. Even so, it nearly did not survive into the 1970s. The 747 had been extremely expensive to produce and orders for the plane were dwindling.

NEW PRODUCTS

Missiles

After World War II, the powerful nations of the world divided into two opposing camps. One was led by the now disbanded communist Soviet Union, the other by the capitalist United States. A "cold war" developed between them. Both nations stockpiled sophisticated nuclear and other weapons. The threat that either side would use these terrible weapons kept a "balance of power" between them. From 1945 onwards, Boeing built missiles for the US government, among them the giant Minuteman ICBM (intercontinental ballistic missile), shown above, and later airborne cruise missiles.

Into space

Part of the competition with the Soviet Union took the form of the "space race." Sooner or later, a man would land on the moon, and the United States was determined that that man would be an American. Boeing had experience in building missiles and military aircraft, so the company was a natural choice to develop the rockets that would carry astronauts into space. The Saturn rockets used in the project were built by Boeing, as were the Lunar Roving Vehicles, shown left, that explored the moon's surface. More recently Boeing helped develop the Space Shuttle and is working on NASA's Space Station Freedom.

Helicopters

In 1960 Boeing bought a helicopter company. During the war in Vietnam, the United States found helicopters invaluable for transporting men and arms over the dense jungle, and for ferrying the wounded away from battle zones. The V-22, shown right above, is a cross between a helicopter and a turbo-prop aircraft.

The Apollo space program was coming to an end. The future of a new supersonic airliner that was partly funded by the government hung in the balance. Boeing was sliding towards bankruptcy.

Business was so bad that the new company president "T" Wilson decided to reduce costs drastically. During the course of 1970 and 1971, Boeing cut its workforce in the Seattle area alone from 80,400 to 37,200. The effect on the population was so bad that someone erected a billboard that read, "Will the last person leaving Seattle turn out the lights?"

Research and development

Boeing's ability to diversify, to come up with one new product after another, and maintain its research and development program even in the worst of times helped what remained of the company to survive. Because it had so many areas of operation and was not scared to invest money in its creative operations, Boeing had the commercial strength to meet the difficulties.

BUSINESS MATTERS: DIVERSIFICATION

There is a limit to the amount anyone can sell of a single product. Businesses need to expand and often they do so by creating new products or buying other companies to acquire ready-made new products. The widening of a range of business activities is called diversification. Having a range of products helps to spread risk. If one product is doing badly, another might be doing well.

Computer services

In 1970 Boeing set up its Computer Services Division. Its purpose was to support Boeing's other activities – design, engineering, telecommunications, data-processing, stock-control, accounting and so on. Many activities formerly carried out laboriously by trial and error, and by time-consuming calculations, could be carried out by computers in a snap. Because of its own needs, Boeing rapidly became a leader in advanced computer technology – and found that it had a new product to sell, its own skill. Boeing now sells or leases its computer programs and expertise to other companies and organizations. Once again, the US government is a major customer. The CATIA computer system, shown below, was used to develop the 777.

▲ Sixteen launch customers signed up for the 250-ton 777 which took to the air for the first time in June 1993.

Right for the customer

Businesses know from experience what their customers liked or disliked in the past. What every business would like to know is what their customers will like in the future. If they knew that, they could design and produce exactly the right products.

When Boeing manufactures equipment to order for the US military or for NASA, it normally gets a strict specification. At other times it might have to produce new designs and estimates in competition with other manufacturers. When it makes civil aircraft, it has to satisfy consumers, the airlines' customers. As well as making sure that its planes are safe and comfortable, it has to make sure that they are the right size and the right price.

▶ The 767-300 is an extended version of the 767. It carries up to 325 passengers and is much in demand with package-tour operators.

BUSINESS MATTERS: RESEARCH

Businesses conduct research to make sure they make the right decisions. Big companies like Boeing and major airlines employ specialists to do the research for them. The research organization asks people to fill out questionnaires or interviews them to find out their likes and dislikes. For an airline survey, they might choose a sample of potential customers, for example, business people or tourists who fly on a particular route. From their answers the researchers will be able to identify the most common needs and concerns.

Changing needs change planes

During the 1970s and 1980s there were increases in fuel prices which forced up air fares and led to general business recessions. The result was a reduction in the number of passengers. Many jumbo jets were flying half empty. Boeing realized that there was a large market for smaller, more fuel-efficient planes, and produced the 757 (to replace the 727) and 767 to meet the need.

Now air traffic looks set to rise again and Boeing has rolled out the 777, the world's largest twin-engined jetliner, destined to become the first of a whole new family of aircraft. It was designed entirely by computer. It is cheaper to run than the huge jumbo jets and carries more passengers than other twin-jets. It is cleaner and less noisy. Even before it flew, Boeing had advance orders from 16 customers for 150 planes.

Responding to customers

Because the 777 will probably be in service for decades, Boeing had to make sure that the plane was right for its customers – the airlines. They took notice of criticisms that airline staff and passengers had made of some features of other Boeing aircraft. More than 100 modifications devised by British Airways staff were adopted, for example. All Nippon Airways and United Airlines also modified the design.

The cost of research and development

Back in the 1950s Boeing risked $20 million developing the 707, an enormous sum in those days. The 747 cost over $1 billion, the 777 probably cost $4 billion. Boeing annually spends $800 million on research and development. The company knows that the price is not too high if it is to stay ahead of the competition.

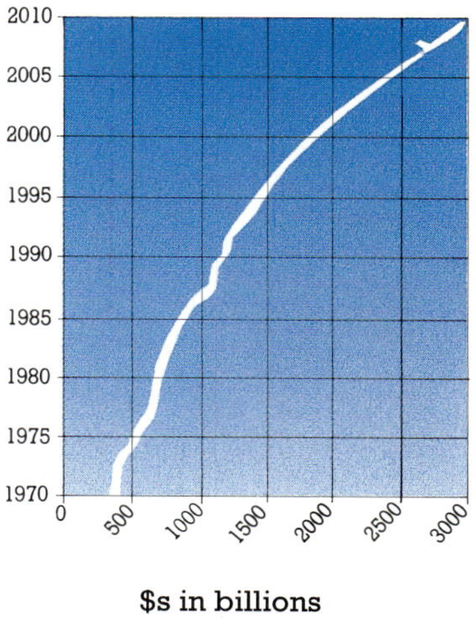

▲ Boeing forecasts that the total world revenue from passenger airlines will rise steadily into the next century.

◀ The 777 can carry 300 or more people over 11,200 km (7,000 miles). Passengers may enjoy interactive videos with a choice of numerous films and TV channels, computer games, video shopping by credit card, and a hotel and car booking service. The first class cabin (inset) and business class cabins will have satellite communications, phones, faxes and computer links.

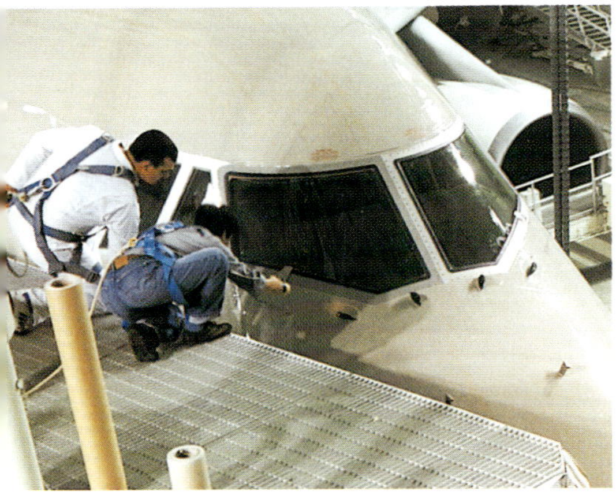

▲ Preparing for painting and applying the paint to an aircraft is a skilled job. New technologies deliver the paint more effectively than in the past. This reduces the time it takes to paint a plane and helps protect staff from the health risks associated with paints and solvents.

The people behind the planes

Imagine all the different tasks to be done in a company like Boeing. There are about 10,000 separate types of job, from managers and engineers, to test pilots, telephonists and catering staff. More than 116,000 people work for the company, and of these nearly 87,000 are based around Boeing's home town of Seattle.

BUSINESS MATTERS: DIVISION OF LABOR

To run efficiently, a company must be properly organized. Any large organization needs to be split into manageable groups. Each of Boeing's divisions, for example, is split into smaller divisions that carry out specialized tasks or operations. The work of each division is further divided, right down to the person who installs the reading lights in an airliner passenger cabin. This system is called division of labor. Instead of one person building a whole aircraft, thousands of specialists create individual parts that can be put together by a fitter. This is an efficient way of working but it can be boring for the person who has to perform the same task over and over, all day every day.

BUSINESS MATTERS: HUMAN RESOURCES

Sometimes called human resources, the people who work for a company are its greatest asset. Once thousands of people were needed to do unskilled or manual jobs. Now jobs can be done by machines and the machines can be controlled by computers. There is less demand for unskilled workers but more for people with talents and skills. That is why it is important for people looking for jobs to train and realize their full potential.

Choosing employees

Boeing seeks to attract and keep the best qualified staff. At the same time it makes sure that it gives equal opportunity to all candidates. Women, members of ethnic and religious minorities, people with disabilities and people of any age are encouraged to take jobs with the company.

Motivation and rewards

Although all companies like to keep their wage bill as low as possible, they recognize that it makes sense to pay people well. It is a waste of time and money to train people and then have them take their experience to another company. Boeing pays about $6 billion every year in wages and salaries. An employee's pay includes health insurance, savings, and pension-plan contributions.

Employees have good opportunities for training and improving their skills. Departments are organized so that people work as a team. Problems are aired, shared and worked on. Staff are kept informed of divisional and company goals so that they know what their role is in the total organization. This helps them to take a pride in their work, and see what is in line for them.

Trade unions

A large proportion of Boeing's workers belong to trade unions that represent their interests. With so many employees, disputes are bound to arise, and Boeing's workers have occasionally gone on strike for better pay and conditions. In 1989 about 57,000 workers belonging to the machinists' union held a 48-day strike that seriously disrupted production and reduced profits. In the end more favorable employment contracts were negotiated with the machinists and with other employees.

◀ Boeing employs more and more skilled staff and fewer and fewer unskilled workers. The company has to train its own staff, especially in computer skills.

BUSINESS MATTERS: LABOR RELATIONS

The employees of any large company often feel that they need an organization that represents their interests. They belong to a trade union. The elected officers of the union meet with the management to set rates of pay, working hours and other conditions of employment. Traditionally, relations between employers and unions have not always been friendly. Some big companies in the United States refuse to deal with unions and will not employ union members. In the aircraft industry, however, there is a high proportion of skilled workers and good rates of pay, so managements and unions have usually worked well together.

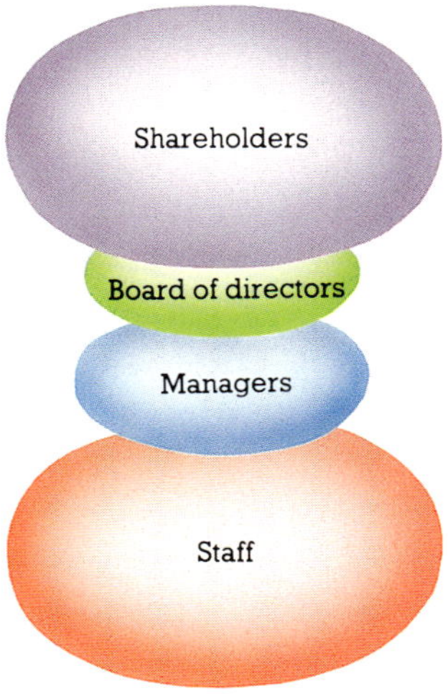

▲ The board of directors is answerable to the shareholders. The management and staff are answerable to the board.

How Boeing manages

Public companies like Boeing are owned by their shareholders. The people who run the company – the directors and management – answer to the shareholders. The shareholders have a right to vote on decisions that affect the company as a whole but they leave the day-to-day running of the business to the board of directors.

The board of directors

A board is another name for a table. The directors of a company sit around a "board" to discuss company affairs. The board is led by a chairman or chairwoman, who is the head, or chief executive, of the company. He or she may also be the president of the company, who is also sometimes called the managing director. Other members of the board represent different divisions of the company, the financial and legal departments, sales and promotions, personnel and company organization, and the operating divisions.

▲ Frank Shrontz is chairman and chief executive of Boeing. He is a lawyer who has spent time with the US Department of Defense and the US Air Force. He is responsible for the present company structure.

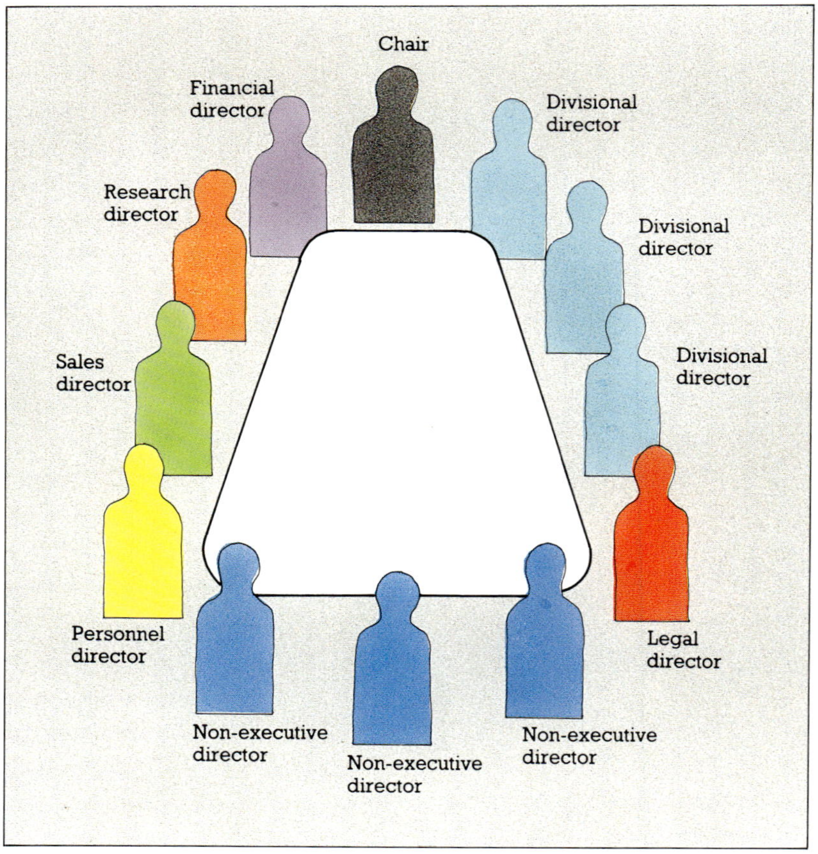

▶ A typical board of directors of a large company. In smaller companies directors may have more than one role. In very small companies there may be only one director.

BUSINESS MATTERS: DIRECTORS

The directors who work for a company are called executive directors. Large companies also have non-executive directors. These are usually directors who work for other companies, such as banks, insurance companies, airlines or other industries. They help the executive directors make decisions. Because they are not involved in the running of the company, they are able to give unbiased advice. They also make sure that the executive directors and chief executive are up to scratch. It might be difficult for junior members of the board to criticize the head of the firm who is their boss. Non-executive directors can do so more easily, so their role is important.

▶ **Managers have an important role in any business. In little over a year, these Boeing team leaders managed to cut 12,000 hours of unnecessary work from one assembly process.**

The managers

The chairman of the company delegates responsibility for carrying out the board's decisions and overseeing the various divisions to the corporate officers, who are also called vice-presidents. The corporate officers in their turn pass some responsibility on to senior managers, who delegate some of their responsibility to junior managers who supervise the employees on the shop floor. Managing a big company is rather like running a military campaign. Command is passed down through a chain of command from the general to the ranks of ordinary soldiers.

BUSINESS MATTERS: MANAGERS

Managers carry out the wishes of the directors and take charge of the staff. They see that work is done on time and in ways that do not cost too much money. They have to make sure that the staff can carry out their tasks efficiently, and that they are confident and happy in their work. They can do this by offering them as much responsibility as they are capable of handling, training them, paying them well and promoting them. No matter how good a company's workers are, they cannot perform well with a poor management.

Money matters

Like any other business person, William Boeing created his company to make money. In the early days he was able to keep the company in business only because he had capital from his other business. People without money of their own have to borrow money from banks or from investors. Over a period of time the borrowed money must be paid back with interest or part of the profits of the company must be paid to investors. If the business does not make money, the debts cannot be repaid.

Cash flow

Sometimes a business fails because it is unable to pay its costs or debts on time. It has problems with its cash flow. Money is entering and leaving the business at the wrong time. The company may have a wonderful product and expect healthy sales in the future, but if there is not enough cash to pay for the staff salaries, raw materials and other costs, the company will be in trouble and may be forced into bankruptcy.

BUSINESS MATTERS: KEEPING ACCOUNTS

It is vital to keep track of money going in and out of a company. To avoid cash flow problems companies need to be able to predict how much they will spend and how much they are likely to earn in the future, and they need to know precisely how much they have spent and how much they have earned.

Every year, all public companies produce an annual report. This document explains to shareholders how the company is getting on. It includes a summary of the company accounts.

The most important part of the accounts is the profit and loss account. It details how much money the company has earned from sales and investments, what its costs were and what its assets are worth.

The difference between the costs and the income is the company's profit. If a company earns more than it spends, it makes a profit. If it spends more than it earns, it makes a loss.

BUSINESS MATTERS: BANKRUPTCY

Bankruptcy is a legal term. When a person or a business is unable to pay their debts they are declared bankrupt by a court. When a business is failing it may ask to be declared bankrupt, to go into voluntary liquidation. If the company cannot be saved, its assets are sold – put into liquidation – and distributed to the creditors (those owed money). Tax and banking debts are paid in full, if possible, and anything left is then shared out. If a business fails to pay its debts, creditors may ask the courts to put the company into involuntary liquidation.

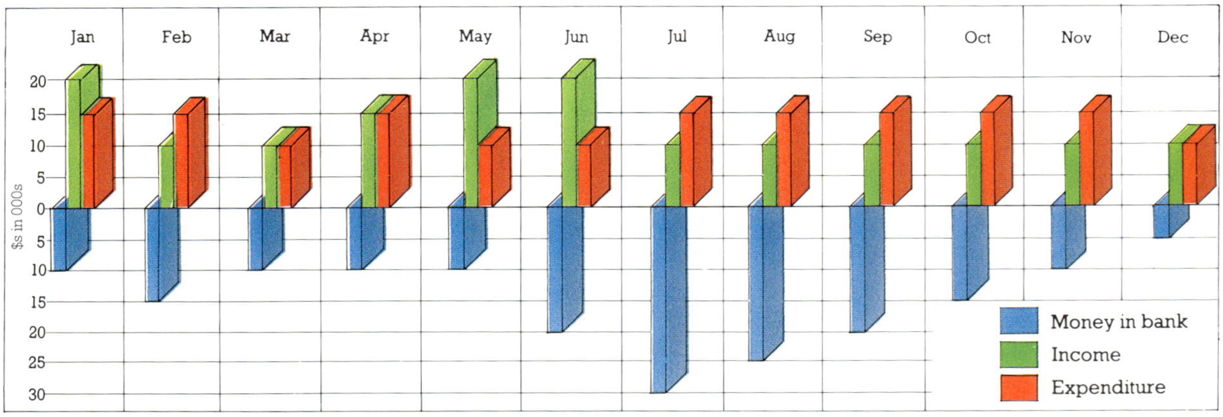

BUSINESS MATTERS: TAXES

A company cannot keep all the profit it makes. It has to pay taxes, just as an individual pays taxes on his or her income. Profit before tax is called gross profit. Profit after tax is called net profit. One way that a company can reduce the amount of tax it pays is by giving money to charities. This benefits the company because it earns good will and publicity. The government, in turn, does not lose out because charitable donations from businesses help reduce the nation's welfare bill.

▶ When customers pay in advance for their aircraft, Boeing makes sure that it gets their specification absolutely right. Here, amid sections of AWACS radar domes, a representative of the Royal Air Force discusses the purchase of the aircraft for Britain.

Investment

Many private companies have investors who own a share in the company. Public companies trade their shares on the stock exchange. When companies want to expand by developing new projects or by buying other companies, they may need even more money. They can raise this by borrowing, issuing more shares or by asking their customers to help them. Boeing has billions of dollars of accumulated profit and yet has borrowings of over $300 million. It also invests in other companies.

◀ Cash flow can be a problem even for normally profitable companies. If this company had not made so much money in the first half of the year, and in the previous year, it would have been in trouble in the second half.

Customer financing

Boeing does not use its borrowings for new projects. It finances major developments from its profits. Airlines that want to order planes or take an option on unbuilt aircraft also make an advance payment. The development of the new 777 was paid for in this way.

Buying and building

When William Boeing founded his company, planes were made of wood. With his expertise in the timber trade, Boeing was able to secure the raw material he needed at the right price. Today planes are made of aluminium and a host of other components. The company also has to buy millions of other items from trucks to telephones that are needed to run the business.

It is important for businesses to be able to depend on their suppliers. For this reason, large companies often buy a share in

▲ The Sheet Metal Center at Auburn, Washington, employs computer-controlled machines to make up to 11 million parts per year.

▶ A technician uses automated equipment to test flight-control systems on a 747-400. Computer-aided tests save time and increase reliability.

the businesses that provide them with essential supplies. This gives them enough control to prevent them being left without vital components or having price increases forced upon them.

Organizing the purchase of so many supplies is extremely complicated. The business has to order and negotiate the right price for each item. It has to make sure that the right quantity of goods is delivered to the right place at the right time. The goods have to be checked and stored and paid for.

Manufacturing

To assemble the 747, Boeing built the world's largest building – in terms of volume – at Everett, Washington. Inside it, 11 cranes, weighing 30 tons each, moved sections of the plane about. It took 21 months to build a jumbo. Nowadays, production time for all Boeing's products is far shorter. Computerized design has reduced design errors and time between design and production. A new Aircraft Systems Laboratory allows new systems to be checked before test flights. There is less manual labour involved and more automation.

▲ Solid-modelling software allows teams of people to work together on any aspect of the design of a new aircraft or system.

BUSINESS MATTERS: PAYING THE BILLS

Most businesses give credit for the goods they sell. This means that they do not demand prior or immediate payment, but give the customer a certain amount of time in which to pay for the goods. Many small businesses get into difficulty because they have to pay their suppliers promptly but do not receive prompt payment for the goods they supply. Some companies have a policy of leaving it as late as possible to pay bills, so that they effectively get free credit. The smaller companies whose goods or services they have already used often find themselves with not enough money to pay their staff and other creditors, and end up bankrupt as a result.

DESIGN BY COMPUTER

Development of the 777 used computer-aided three-dimensional interactive application (CATIA) software, a digital graphics system. Using thousands of CATIA workstations, engineers designed and assembled the parts of the aircraft on screen and worked out the exact sizes and shapes of the sections and components before they were manufactured and assembled. All the parts fitted perfectly.

Prime contractor

Aerospace manufacturing is so complex, that it is almost impossible for one company to undertake a large project alone. So nowadays several companies collaborate. The company that controls the operation is called the team leader, or prime contractor. Boeing has used this system to develop several products, including major defense and space projects. At present Boeing is acting as prime contractor for the building of NASA's permanent space station Freedom with partners from Europe, Japan, Canada and Russia.

▲ Ready for action, a helicopter touches down in the desert – or does it? This is only a realistic model of Boeing's new RAH-66 Comanche helicopter on show to the US army and other customers.

▶ Ready for take-off? No, just a mock-up of the passenger cabin of the 777 for customers to evaluate.

BUSINESS MATTERS: ADVERTISING

Advertising is a way of showing a company's products or services to people. Businesses pay to advertise in the media – on television, in magazines and newspapers and on billboards. Companies such as Boeing do not need to advertise to the general public. They target their customers, airlines and armed forces around the world, by placing ads in trade journals and sending promotional literature to them by direct mail. The airlines, however, want the public as a whole to know about them, so they advertise in all the media.

Selling the goods

In order to keep its 60 per cent share of the civil aircraft market, Boeing has to look after its customers. It knows from experience exactly who its potential customers are, and who its competitors are. It has to sell itself and its planes continuously, and get its major customers involved from the start. It would be far too risky to build an aircraft on the off-chance of it selling.

Long before a new model goes into production, Boeing starts selling it. It sends detailed information to airlines and may arrange conferences where interested parties can question designers and engineers. It also produces sophisticated video presentations using models. Its specially trained sales force visits customers to explain the technological details and answer questions knowledgeably. Big customers are entertained at Boeing headquarters and shown every detail to satisfy them

that their needs will be met. Later the company will advertise in aviation trade journals and provide information and interviews to aviation writers.

The finished product

Once Boeing has sufficient commitments from the airlines, the aircraft goes into production. A prototype undergoes strict trials and test flights. As the plane rolls out, the publicity machine rolls out with it. The rollout itself is a media event attended by journalists and customers, as well as a celebration for all the people who built the plane.

BUSINESS MATTERS: PUBLICITY

Publicity is not paid for directly by companies, though most companies put effort and money into trying to secure good publicity for themselves. They might wine and dine newspaper editors or journalists in the hope of persuading them to feature their company or product. They send out press releases with news stories that might fill a space in the newspaper. An article in a paper about the company or the product may be worth more than a paid-for ad. Sometimes, however, publicity is harmful to a company. If an aircraft crashed and the media said it was because of poor design or work, the company that made it would suffer.

▲ Boeing provides customers with maintenance and engineering support in 56 countries. Here a field service engineer is on hand to deal with any problems as an aircraft turns round in the Cayman Islands.

◀ Boeing trains an average of 6,000 pilots and ground personnel each year. Here an Air France captain receives instruction in a 747-400 simulator.

After-sales service

Boeing cannot just sell its products and forget about them. It has to make sure that pilots and crews around the world know how to operate the planes, and that spare parts and service are continuously available. Some aircraft are in service for 30 years or more and may be sold by one customer to another. During all this time Boeing takes responsibility for overseeing their maintenance and care.

▲ Boeing employees are well known for the voluntary work they do in the community. The company provides equipment and supplies but the staff give their time and care free.

The Boeing image

Just as individuals care about their appearance and what people think of them, so companies worry about their image. Boeing knows the value of good publicity and of good public relations. It has an image as an international company and as a national and local company.

Spreading good will

Boeing is a highly profitable company. It reinvests much of the money it makes in the company, pays some to its shareholders and some as tax to the government. And every year it gives millions of dollars away to charity. In 1994 the company contributed more than $60 million to a wide range of community programs in support of education, health and human service programs. Boeing staff contributed several million hours of their own time to community service.

Good neighbor

In Seattle and other places where it operates, Boeing looms large in the daily lives of the local people. Many work directly for Boeing and thousands of others work in organizations that supply goods or services to the company. Boeing makes sure that people think of it as an organization that benefits the community. As well as providing jobs, it gives valuable help to local organizations, either by giving cash or gifts of computers and printing facilities. This provides much-prized good publicity.

▼ Catching them young! Boeing gives financial, technological and leadership support in public education.

◀ A teacher financed by Boeing helps children with a dinosaur project in a Washington State school. It isn't all high-tech!

EDUCATION

Two-thirds of Boeing's educational aid – $10 million in 1993 – goes to universities and colleges, and the rest to primary and vocational education projects. The company believes that improving the quality of education for young children will improve the quality of older students. People who benefit may well look on Boeing as a future employer and will no doubt always feel grateful to the company.

Protecting the planet and its people

Boeing is committed to providing a safe and healthy working environment for its staff and a safe environment for the world. Air pollution from the poisonous chemicals in the paints and solvents used in the manufacture of aircraft are monitored and minimized. Solid waste is recycled where possible.

Aircraft in the air can be noisy and dirty. They offload fuel in the skies and damage the ozone layer and the environment. The noise they make causes hardship to thousands of people. Concern with pollution, and controls to regulate it, have persuaded Boeing to undertake research in collaboration with the US government into ways of making aircraft cleaner and quieter. It also belongs to other organizations dedicated to protecting the environment and the ozone layer.

DOLLAR FOR DOLLAR

As well as giving hours of their own time to help local causes, Boeing's workers give to many charitable programs through its Good Neighbor Fund. The company matches part of the staff charitable donations by an equal amount, doubling the total donation.

◀ Paint delivered through this special spray-gun is drawn to the surface of the aircraft. This makes for fewer harmful paint particles in the air and therefore less risk to the workers' health.

Competition

Boeing's position as America's top aerospace company has not been seriously challenged since the 1950s, but rival companies have kept it on its toes. Its greatest rivals in the United States have been Douglas (now McDonnell-Douglas) and Lockheed. The European consortium Airbus Industrie has been a rival to all three companies since the 1970s.

Getting ahead

Technical excellence and good business management have been the key to Boeing's ability to stay ahead of its rivals. It has also learned from experience. In the early 1930s Boeing lost out to Douglas because it could not supply enough 247s to meet the demand. Since then it has always made sure that it had the capacity to deliver.

In the 1970s jet technology was not new; it was openly available. But to build a long-haul jet airliner demanded a huge investment. The cost was so high that Boeing knew that it could not share the potential market for it. The company was so scared of its rivals stealing a march on it, that it built the new 707 in secret.

In the 1960s all three American companies sought to secure a contract to build a gigantic military transport plane. Boeing lost the contract, but it was partly able to make use of the design and technology it had developed to create the 747.

▲ Lockheed's C5 Galaxy. Boeing failed to win the contract for this huge cargo plane, but its research work was not wasted. It was used to develop the 747.

◀ The A300 Airbus. Airbus Industrie's new A340 is in direct competition with Boeing's new 777. Boeing considers this competition unfair because some of the airbus manufacturers receive government subsidies.

▲ Because of fears of environmental damage, Concorde, the Anglo-French SST, was not allowed to land at New York or most other US airports.

Lockheed, who won the order, overran its budget in building the winning C5 Galaxy and had to be saved from bankruptcy by the government. Its L1011 TriStar jumbo jet was unable to compete with the 747, and it now no longer makes commercial airliners.

Staying ahead

Unable to compete with giant American companies on their own, aircraft manufacturers from four European countries banded together to develop the A300 Airbus. Launched in 1972, sales of the Airbus were initially slow, perhaps because nobody could believe that Europe could match or outstrip American aircraft design. But the airbus and its successors eventually took a fairly large slice of the market.

With the development of the 777, Boeing hopes to reduce the share of the market that Airbus Industrie gained with its A330 and A340 medium-sized long-range jets.

BUSINESS MATTERS: COMPETITION AND CHOICE

Competition benefits the consumer. If consumers have a choice of product, the businesses competing for their custom have an incentive to keep quality high and prices low. To keep prices low, they have to manage their companies well, cut out waste and make the business as cost effective as possible.

Sometimes large companies seek to rid themselves of all competition. They lower their prices so far that rival firms are put out of business. This then gives them a monopoly. Fortunately, there are laws against such practices in most countries.

On government orders

▶ The B-2 bomber is based on the "flying wing" concept, and is nearly invisible to radar. Boeing was a key member of the team of companies, led by Northrop, that built it.

▲ The IUS (Inertial Upper Stage) is used with the US Air Force's Titan rockets and the Space Shuttle. Its job will be to place satellites in orbits that the Shuttle cannot reach and even to travel to other planets and into solar orbit.

Any company that wants to build military aircraft or weapons has to work closely with their government, otherwise their work would be illegal and dangerous. Military projects generally cost a great deal of money, they must conform to exact specifications and some must be built in secret. Because government contracts are so important, manufacturers go to great lengths to secure them. But working on military contracts is also a risky business, as Boeing has repeatedly found to its cost. Wars end and contracts are cancelled.

At the end of the 1980s, the "cold war" came to an end and the US government reduced or cancelled orders for new aircraft and air defense systems. Boeing found itself making a loss in that area of operations. Fortunately the profits made elsewhere were enough to cover the shortfall.

GOVERNMENT PROJECTS

CH-47 Chinook helicopter

* **Early years**
  Military trainers and flying boats for the US Navy and fighters for the US Army.
* **1930s & 1940s**
  B-17 Flying Fortress (1935) and B-29 Superfortress (1942) bombers; B-29 "Enola Gay" drops atom bomb on Hiroshima (1945). Work begins on ground-to-air pilotless aircraft (1946). B-47 Stratojet bomber (1947).
* **1950s**
  B-52 Stratofortress (prototype 1952). Bomarc missile (1952). KC-135 military tanker (1954). Work begins on SST. First Air Force One delivered (1959).
* **1960s**
  Launch of Minuteman ICBM (1961). Vertol's Ch-47A Chinook helicopter begins service in Vietnam (1961). Work begins on Saturn V booster rocket for Apollo Program (1961). B-52s start bombing North Vietnam in operation Rolling Thunder (1965). Work begins on SRAM (short-range attack missiles) and lunar orbiters which are to survey moon landing sites (1966). Boeing rocket boosters and systems integration play vital role in successful moon landing.
* **1970s**
  Lunar Roving Vehicles (1971). Government funding for SST cancelled(1971). Wins contract to design hydrofoil patrolboats equipped with missiles for the navy (1971). Begins work on Mariner 10 Venus spaceprobe (1971). Begins work on ALCM – air-launched cruise missile (1972). E-3A AWACS starts work as spy plane (1976).
* **1980s**
  B-2 Stealth bomber (1980). Inertial Upper Stage (IUS) space vehicle boosts Magellan and Galileo craft towards Venus and Jupiter. Awarded contract for "star wars" Peace Shield (1985). E-6A VLF (Very Low Frequency) Communications System (1987). V-22 Osprey tiltrotor helicopter's first flight (1989).
* **1990s**
  New 747-200 Air Force One delivered. Prime contractor for Space Station Freedom. Avenger air defence program continues. Upgraded B-52H bomber delivered late 1993 for tests by US Air Force.

F-22 Fighter

Change of policy

Governments change from time to time and what suits one political party does not suit another. In some countries even civil aircraft manufacturers are subsidized by their governments. Unsubsidized manufacturers, such as Boeing, have to compete with their products. Boeing spent years developing an SST (supersonic transport plane), partly funded by the government, but in the end the project was cancelled. The research and technology will probably not be wasted, but used to develop Boeing's new supersonic civil aircraft.

The future

Throughout its history Boeing has had to adapt to cope with alternating periods of peace and war, recession and boom. In the second half of the 1990s, airline traffic is set to rise by over five per cent per year. Boeing has estimated that the total commercial airplane market will be worth $460 billion and it aims to have the largest share of it. On the other hand, the break-up of the Soviet Union has forced the US and other western governments to look again at many of their military projects, including those being handled by Boeing.

Boeing's aim for the future is continuous improvement in the quality of products and processes. The company is determined to cut waste and boost productivity so that it can produce higher quality products in less time at the lowest possible cost. The use of sophisticated computer technology has helped reduce costs and production times.

▼ After research into noise and fuel technology, Boeing is confident that the High-Speed Civil Transport will not have the same drawbacks as Concorde and the Soviet Union's Tupolev Tu-144.

Change

For 80 years Boeing has kept ahead of its rivals by always looking ahead and planning for the future. It has taken risks that have not always paid off. It has sometimes been unsuccessful in the short term but successful in the long term. When one market closed, it found or made new ones. Its fame and its success have depended on the achievements of its designers and engineers. With modern technology available to them, there is no knowing what advances the company will make in the future.

WHAT NEXT?

▲ **Getting ready for 2001, Space Station Freedom will be the first international orbiting laboratory.**

The commercial future

The 777, which rolled out in 1994, already looks like a winner. The first of three Next-Generation 737 Series models is due for delivery in 1997. Together with potential international partners, research is under way on the prospects for an airplane larger than the 747-400, an airplane smaller than the current 737-500, and the next-generation supersonic jet-liner.

Defense

Even in peacetime, countries have to make sure that they have enough up-to-date equipment to defend themselves and to defend their weaker allies. At Boeing work proceeds on more B-2 Stealth bombers, on the 767 AWACS, on the missile-based Avenger air-defense system, on the Bell-Boeing V-22 Osprey tiltrotor, and on many other projects, some of them secret.

Space

Boeing is well advanced in NASA's ambitious project to put a permanent space station called Freedom into space. The company is designing and building the living laboratory and support modules of the craft. It is also continuing to manufacture the Inertial Upper Stage (IUS) booster rocket. This rocket takes a satellite from the space shuttle on to its operational orbit and launches probes into deeper space. In 1990 it launched the European Space Agency sun probe Ulysses.

Computer services

The Computer Services Division will continue to support all of Boeing's operations, making tremendous cost savings and great contributions to Boeing's earnings by the sale of its services to the government, armed services, and private concerns. It installs large-scale information networks tailored to particular customers' needs.

Create your own business

◀ Fly a kite! Create interest in your product by letting your customers see a prototype at work.

Boeing makes money by selling a vast range of goods and services. It started by making only one. See if you can run a business making and selling a new product.

Choose a product that you can make cheaply and easily, and sell to friends and neighbors. A kite would be a good idea. You could use your pocket money to make one kite, sell it and use the profit to make another, but you will probably make more money if you make lots of similar kites. You will be able to buy materials more cheaply and you will be able to spread many of the costs over several kites. Get some friends to come in with you, or ask if you can do the project at school.

Management

Select a small team to manage your kite company: someone to look after the money, someone to do the design, people to make the kites, do the publicity, selling and so on.

Capital

You will need money to buy raw materials. If everyone contributes some of their own money, they will find their parents more willing to lend some. You must return investors' money with interest.

Planning

Decide what you want to do. Think about your customers. Who will you be selling to? What sort of kite would best suit them? How much will they be willing to pay? How many customers will there be? Do some research. Estimate the maximum numbers of kites you can sell and the minimum. What is the likely number?

The product

What makes your kite worth buying? Check the competition. Shop-bought kites might be superior, but you may be able to make and sell yours for less money. Yours might be more expensive but better made. Make sure you know what your customers want. Think about Boeing's attitude towards research, design and technology.

▲ Remember what you need – capital, raw materials, labor, equipment and marketing.

PROFIT AND LOSS ACCOUNT		
Sales		400.00
Less cost of sales		
Paper	20.00	
Wood	75.00	
Glue	5.00	
Design	30.00	
	130.00	130.00
Gross profit		270.00
Less overhead		
Rent	5.00	
Wages	30.00	
Stationery	10.00	
Video camera rental	30.00	
	75.00	75.00
Net profit		195.00
Loan repayment	100.00	
Interest	5.00	
Net profit after interest		90.00

▲ Proper businesses present their figures as a profit and loss account like this.

Costing

When you have done your research, see if your venture will work financially. How much will you have to pay to produce, advertise, sell and distribute your product? Remember your "overhead" – extra items like bus fares, stationery and postage.

Add up all the costs. Work out how many items you must sell to cover your costs and get back all the money you have spent. This is your break-even point: anything less and you make a loss, anything more and you make a profit. Work out your profit per item.

Selling

If you get your customers to order and pay partly for their kites in advance, you will lessen the financial risk you are taking. To attract interest from the market, you might consider making a prototype kite so that people can see what they will be buying and let you know if there are special features they require. You also need to advertise your kites. Perhaps you could make a kite commercial on the school video recorder. You could place an ad in the school magazine and posters on the noticeboards. Drum up publicity as well. Ask the local paper to run a story. Stage a kite-flying competition at the local park.

Production

Give everyone on the project a definite job. Divide up the tasks of kite-making – putting the frame together, putting the paper on, making the tail, and so on. Choose people who are good at each task. This will speed production.

Profit and loss

Keep a record of what you spend and what you receive. If you have made a lot of profit, you will need to pay your investors and then decide what to do with the rest of the money. Should you split it amongst yourselves, give some to charity or your school (if you were a real company, you would have to pay tax on your profits), or put your profits back into the business? You could buy more raw materials for kites or a new product. What would Boeing do?

The language of business

Accountant Person who keeps or inspects accounts.
Accounts Records that show money going in or out of a business.
Advertising Making publicly known. Advertisers use television, radio, newspapers and so on to tell everyone how good their product or service is.
Aerospace Earth's atmosphere and outer space where aircraft and spacecraft fly.
Aluminum Light silvery metal that is combined with other metals to make the alloys from which aircraft bodies and parts are mostly made.
Annual report Published record of a company's accounts and business for the previous year.
Assembly line Series of machines and workers in a factory set up to assemble a product in a sequence of tasks.
Assets Anything owned by a business including property, money, goods and machines.
Automation Manufacture of a product using machines rather than people.
Bankrupt Having no money in the bank or any means of paying debts.
Billion A thousand million or, in Britain, a million million. Billions in this book are a thousand million.
Board of directors See Directors.
Boom Time when business is good and customers can afford to buy products.
Break-even The point at which income from sales equals the cost of production and sales.
Business An organization that sells goods or services in return for money.
Capital Money needed to start a business and keep it going.
Capitalist Economic or political system in which private (rather than state) capital is used to produce and distribute goods.
Cash flow The rate at which money enters and leaves a business during any period of time.
Cent See Dollar.
Chairman The person who leads a committee or board of directors. Also called a chairperson or chair.
Chief executive The highest-ranking person in a company who has full power to act and make decisions on behalf of the company.
Choice Variety of products for customers to choose from.
Civil aircraft Non-military aircraft. Also called commercial aircraft.
Commercial To do with trade.
Communism Economic and political system in which the state controls farms, factories and businesses,which are held in common ownership.
Company Organization of a group of people to carry on a business. Companies may be small or large, public or private. See also Corporation.
Competition The struggle for customers and profits between two or more enterprises in the same field.
Consumer The purchaser or user of an article or service. See also Customer.
Corporate officers Senior managers of a corporation. They include the chief executive officer, the president, the executive officers and vice-presidents. In Britain these officers are usually called directors. See Directors.
Corporation Business corporations are usually large, centrally organized public companies.
Costs The amount of capital that it takes to make and sell a product or service; costings are forecasts of those costs.
Credit To give credit is to allow time for a payment to be made. Bookkeepers write down payments as credits, and debts as debits. A creditor is a person or business to whom a business owes money.
Customer Anyone who buys from a seller, especially one who buys regularly. A customer is not necessarily a consumer. Boeing's customers are mostly airlines, their passengers are consumers.
Customer financing A system in which the customer pays part of the price of a product in advance to help finance its production.
Debit See Credit.
Directors People who guide the activities of a company and make its most important decisions. They are members of the board of directors, which is led by the chairman or chief executive. The directors report to the managing director who may also be the chairman of the board. See also Corporate officers.
Diversification The widening of the range of goods and services produced.
Dividend A small part of a company's profits paid to a shareholder in return for his or her investment.
Division of labor A system that splits up the production process so that each worker or group of workers carries out a specialized job.
Dollar Unit of US currency made up of 100 cents. The equivalent in UK pounds at the moment is about 66 pence, but rates of exchange between countries vary all the time.
Earnings Money gained by a person working or by a company selling.
Economy 1 Careful use of resources or reductions in costs. 2 Overall administration of a community's or country's resources.
Employee A person who works for another person or a company in return for a wage or salary.
Employer A person or company who provides work for employees.
Enterprise 1 A business or company. 2 Originality and inventiveness shown by a business person.
Entrepreneur An enterprising person who is willing to take risks.
Environment The surroundings in which people, animals and plants live.
Executive director A director who works for a company. A non-executive director is a member of the board but is not employed by the company. See also Directors.
Financial To do with money.
Financial director An executive responsible for financial planning, making and receiving payments, and keeping records. The finance department includes accountants and bookkeepers.
Goods Things other than food produced by a business.
Gross See Net and gross.
Growth Expansion of a business to increase profits.
Health insurance A method of paying for health care by making regular payments called premiums to an insurance company.

Human resources The people who work for a business. Also called staff or personnel.
Image How a company is seen by the public.
Income The money that an individual or business receives from earnings or investments.
Inflation A general rise in prices.
Interest Money paid to investors for use of the money they have lent.
Invest To put money into a business or buy shares in it. The sum of money invested is called an investment.
Labor A collective name for workers, especially manual workers.
Liquidation The selling of a company's assets for cash.
Loss The money that a business loses when it spends more than it earns.
Manager A person who controls or organizes a business or part of it. A person who organizes staff.
Managing director See Directors.
Manufacturer A business that makes or produces goods.
Market The total number of buyers and sellers of a product.
Market research Surveying people's tastes and requirements to assess the demand for a product.
Media The means by which a message is transmitted, including newspapers, radio and television.
Merger The joining of two or more companies to form a new one.
Mock-up An experimental model that shows what the final product will look like.
Modification Alteration.
Monopoly Possession of sole control over the selling of a particular product or service.
Net and gross A gross amount is money paid or earned before tax and other contributions have been deducted to leave a net amount.
Non-executive director See Executive director.
Overheads General costs, such as rent, heating, stationery and so on, that do not relate to a specific operation or item.
Ozone A form of the gas oxygen. A layer of ozone in the atmosphere protects us from the sun's harmful ultraviolet radiation. It can be damaged by pollution.
Package-tour operator Travel agent who sells organized holidays, usually involving chartered flights.
Pension plan A method of saving money to provide a retirement income. Often both employers and employees contribute.
Physical resources Things such as buildings, machines and raw materials that a business uses.
Pioneer The first person to explore new territory or start a venture.
Pollution The spoiling of the environment by poisonous gases and other harmful substances, or by noise.
Price The amount of money for which something can be bought or sold. Price is usually determined by supply and demand.
Prime contractor The company in charge of all the other companies in a joint project.
Private company A company that is owned by an individual or group of individuals, and whose shares are not traded on the stock exchange. See also Public company.
Product The thing that a business sells. Products can be goods or services.
Profit The difference between what a company earns – its income – and its costs.
Profit and loss account Part of the accounts that shows what profit or loss a company has made over a certain period.
Promotion 1 Moving up the employment scale to a better job. 2 Promoting sales by advertising, publicity and other sales incentives such as giveaway items.
Prototype A trial model or first version of a product.
Public company A business that offers shares of itself for sale to the general public.
Publicity News or information about a company's activities and products.
Raw materials The ingredients needed to make a product.
Recession A time of unfavorable economic conditions when demand for goods is low.
Research Investigating new developments in design, technology and other fields. See also Market research.
Risk To invest money which may be lost.
Rollout Launch of a new aircraft.
Salary Money paid in fixed amounts, usually monthly, to "white-collar" workers.
Sales forecast Estimate of the likely number of sales to be made during a given period, based on experience and market conditions.
Senior vice-president See Corporate officers.
Service Providing help rather than goods.
Shareholder A person who owns shares in a company.
Shares Tiny portions of a company's capital value. The price at which shares are bought and sold goes up and down according to the company's success. See also Stock.
Specification The detailed description of a product to be manufactured, often provided by the customer.
Sponsorship Providing money or other assistance for sporting, charitable or cultural events.
Staff All the people who work for a company, or workers other than the management.
State control Regulation of industry and other areas by the government.
Stock 1 Products stored ready for sale by a company. Also called inventory in the US. 2 A block of shares.
Stock market Exchange where stocks and shares are bought and sold. Also called a stock exchange.
Stockholder Person who holds stock.
Subsidiary A business controlled by another business. It may be partly or wholly owned.
Subsidy Money paid by a government or other body to manufacturers to keep the price of products low.
Supersonic Faster than the speed of sound.
Supplier Company or individual that supplies raw materials or components to another.
Tax Money that businesses and individuals have to pay the government from their earnings.
Trade union Associations formed by workers to improve their conditions and wages.
Vice-president Person responsible to a senior vice-president or to the board of directors for work done by people under his or her supervision.
Wage Weekly payment of hourly rate paid to "blue-collar" (manual) workers.

Index

Numbers in *italics* indicate pictures and diagrams; those in **bold** indicate panel references.

PRINTED IN BELGIUM BY proost INTERNATIONAL BOOK PRODUCTION